SOUTH BEACH

Art Deco to Contemporary

architectural photographs

Paul Clemence

Schiffer Publishing Ltd®

4880 Lower Valley Road, Atglen, PA 19310 USA

Library of Congress Cataloging-in-Publication Data

Clemence, Paul.
  South Beach architectural photographs : art deco to contemporary / by Paul
    Clemence. p. cm.
  ISBN 0-7643-2086-6 (hardcover)
  1. Architecture—Florida—South Beach (Miami Beach)—Pictorial works. 2. South
Beach (Miami Beach, Fla.)—Pictorial works. 3. Miami Beach (Fla.)—Pictorial works. 4.
Architectural photography—Florida—South Beach (Miami Beach) I. Title.
NA735.M4C57 2004
720'.9759'381—dc22
                              2004006095

Designed by Joseph M. Riggio Jr.
Type set in Gentle Sans Light

ISBN: 0-7643-2086-6
Printed in China

Published by Schiffer Publishing Ltd.
4880 Lower Valley Road
Atglen, PA 19310
Phone: (610) 593-1777; Fax: (610) 593-2002
E-mail: Info@schifferbooks.com

For the largest selection of fine reference books on this and related subjects, please

visit our web site at www.schifferbooks.com
We are always looking for people to write books on new and related subjects. If you
have an idea for a book please contact us at the above address.

This book may be purchased from the publisher.
Include $3.95 for shipping.
Please try your bookstore first.

You may write for a free catalog.

In Europe, Schiffer books are distributed by
Bushwood Books
6 Marksbury Ave.
Kew Gardens
Surrey TW9 4JF England
Phone: 44 (0) 20 8392-8585; Fax: 44 (0) 20 8392-9876
E-mail: info@bushwoodbooks.co.uk
Free postage in the U.K., Europe; air mail at cost.

For my parents, Denis and Mária, for
all their love, respect, and inspiration!

acknowledgements

First of all, I'd like to thank Michael Hughes for writing such an articulate foreword. Stylish, informative, fun, and historic — your text blends easily with the photos. Thanks for bringing your talent and all your dedication to this project!

To all the text contributors, who generously gave their time and effort, I am deeply grateful! Their wit and insight lend a remarkable character to this book, creating a unique profile of South Beach. Iris, Helene, Steve, Dan, Mauricio, Asandra, Cora, Julie, Bianca, Johan, and Jimmy — THANKS! It's nice to be among friends!

As in a relay race, the baton of support has been mysteriously passed forward throughout the development of this book. First, by Tom Gilfillan, who gives me perspective to see ahead. Then James Mckenzie, always there for me. Enter, Stephen Anderson, the most positive ignitor. After that, my brother Peter Clemence, believing in me at a crucial moment and energizing me with confidence. And finally, at the last stretch, Iris Chase, making my dream possible! Thank you!

For the most interesting, creative, enthusiastic, and productive exchange I'm deeply indebted to two great persons – Mauricio Barrera and Julie Davidow. To Julie, I'm also grateful for her assistance with the task of finishing this book in a very short amount of time.

Along the way, some have always participated, even from afar. My brother Denis Clemence, Fernando Werneck, and Ron Cox. Thank you!

From the start, the following have been important participants in one way or another, and I thank them – Will Crockett, Mary Jane Peace, Herb Sosa, Igor Roa, Ana Lucia Campagnuncio, Moyra Clemence, Frank Tribble, Oscar Alvarez, Boris Falcov, Harvey Stein, Marc Poisson, Gisela Pontes, Charles Falarara, the crew at the Kennedy Gallery, Jairaj Abuvala, Susan Watson, and John Tosi.

To Melissa Cardona, Joe Langman, and Tina Skinner from Schiffer Publishing, thanks for the support and appreciation of my work!

Special thanks to Henry Martin from LIB Photo Lab for all his help and expertise producing most of the prints in this book, and to David Hayes for his assistance with the book cover.

And finally, to Sal, for showing me his beautiful photographs and inspiring me to begin this journey, Thank you!

Paul Clemence

contents

introduction

In any city, architecture is a defining element. Whether it's through its style, inventiveness, or scale, the buildings we see and experience play a big role in how we perceive a place.

Here in South Beach, comprised mostly of a consistent group of buildings, our architecture has an even larger impact. In the next pages we'll visually explore some of the main elements that create such an interesting and unique urban setting.

To add a "voice" to these images, residents and active participants in the community were invited to give their personal views on South Beach. The variety of their perspectives and impressions gives us an idea of how diversified and cosmopolitan this sandbar has become.

I've been living and photographing in this town for 15 years, enjoying and observing it through its incredible evolution. Though there's probably still much more to come, I feel it's safe to say that South Beach is now ready for its close-up!

Enjoy the book!

Paul Clemence

"Tides Side"

foreword

Miami Beach began as a swampy sandbar without a name. A visionary showed up in 1913 determined to build a resort out of it. It has been filled with dream makers and paradise seekers ever since. Each successive generation has reshaped the city in its image, and few regard the built environment as unchangeable.

This is a place where the population has forever been hugely in flux, where only one third of the residents are long term. There is little opportunity for continuity, and we might never think about the dozens of people from all over the world who may have lived in our apartments before us. Yet, remaining all about us and in abundance are the clues of what these people might have enjoyed. They are the doorways and rooflines, windows and urban landscapes that speak volumes for the power of design becoming a personal part of daily life. One delights in looking at them everyday, never dulling on their beauty. They instead become a part of one's personal landscape. Today's forty story buildings take a bit more effort: intimacy isn't part of their equation. As we build 500 feet tall in a place nature only saw fit for a mangrove, we might lose sight of what is right in front of us on the sidewalk.

Paul Clemence has admiringly been looking up and away from the street with his lens to capture the glow of our architectural form. His photographs amuse and captivate as we try to determine the time of day or location, and wonder if we've seen this for ourselves. His clever approach allows us to view his subject buildings in an almost responsive pose to the sun's rays. As a resident of South Beach, he has had the luxury, as I have, of marveling over these structures and their forms at all hours and in every light. Each passing minute creates a new tableau to enjoy as a shadow creeps along a façade.

Like him I have gazed at the roofline of the Tides from the 12th Street beach, or spied the Delano's fins from a nearby corner. These buildings beg to be stared at, enjoyed in a changing light, walked up to and thoroughly examined. During the 1930s, south of Lincoln Road became awash in hotels with delicious details that set each apart from its neighbor. They represented a new chapter in the life of Miami Beach; they were the beacons of the good life, dashing the dread of the Great Depression and lining up along the Atlantic Ocean like beauty queens.

But unlike now, most of these visitors were those with modest incomes, people who merely wanted a fresh breeze and time away from the factory floor. I'd like to think they enjoyed the architecture immensely – it had to be a life's dream, a Miami Beach apartment. Today, we seek far greater pleasures from Miami Beach – its hotels and restaurants cater to demanding clientele who know all the world's destinations and expect to be dazzled. Walking the city, where rows of little buildings all with intriguing details are magnified by an endless blue sky, you are captivated by their originality, modesty, and ability to please. But you have to look at them and imagine them as home.

In addition to the street corner palm trees, flowering tropical plants, glorious warm weather, ocean breezes, and endless water vistas, you realize there is much to enjoy. There may be a lot more building to get your eyes around now, but the remaining views are still cast with entertaining light and shadow, and are something to behold. Miami Beach has a natural and built environment that commands us to take a moment and say, "This is a great place to live." Sure, it is clogged with automobiles and no, not everyone is a model citizen, but take your eye higher as Paul has and stretch a bit. Look up into the buildings and catch a corner against the sky, or set your eyes out to the beach and over the water and discover why, year after year we stay and continue to buy into it, study it, photograph it, cherish it – the town has charms worth investing your soul into.

Our history fascinates me, and when Paul asked me to write something to introduce his photos, the criteria went like this – keep it brief, add some history, and note the concept. Fortunately, Paul and I think alike about Miami Beach, we just approach our enthusiasm differently. For me, I want to get to know our local predecessors intimately and then convey to others some sense of what went on before we arrived. Change, whether it's deemed progress or not, is the sole characteristic that has been ever present here. Paul intuitively picks out his own precise details of our changing surroundings and packages them for us in stark black and white as if the subjects are on dry ice. What he has captured are the intricate details of moderne and streamline architecture. The astounding beauty of this South Beach legacy is unique in American history, for the creators of Art Deco would remake the brand-new-but-old-world-style resort city into a tropical modern one. From the Catskills and Atlantic City came Jewish hoteliers who built these ever-so-clever hotels. They reshaped the city's legacy and, unknown to them, would give us the ticket to our prosperity today.

The development of the South Beach area began during the 1910s when the African-American laborers working for Carl Fisher machined its western edge into existence by pumping bay bottom sand into usable land. Fisher, the auto headlight king of Indianapolis, had money to burn and a vision to create. Before his arrival, the narrow beachfront was an avocado plantation owned by an aging New Jersey Quaker, John Collins, whose family quickly saw the potential of working with Fisher on creating a tourist destination. They, along with the lesser-known Lummus brothers turned a swampy mangrove into a flat, desolate plain of crushed coral ready to build into a modern resort. Land buyers didn't come quickly at first. America was in the throes of the First World War and the earliest settlers were locals who built modest homes mostly centered at our southern tip. A legacy of this era still exists and thrives as only one Miami Beach institution can – from sandwich stand to international sensation, Joe's Stone Crab is older than the city itself.

By the 1920s, the wealthy of the Midwest had arrived, lured by Fisher's gift of promotion. His resort came complete with golf, tennis, polo playing, motor yacht racing, and restrictions on non-Gentile patrons. Much of the area remained undeveloped during this time, each block holding just a handful of buildings. Yesteryear's exclusive polo field is today's everyman's Flamingo Park, bustling with tennis, swimming, soccer, and dog play. Of Fisher's five hotels, none is still standing, and one of his golf courses gave way to the Miami Beach Convention Center. During the 1930s, an unending arrival of a mostly Jewish middle class transformed the South Beach landscape from suburban to urban. While the nation experienced the Great Depression, here we became the triumph of capitalism. Retirees, vacationers, developers, and dreamers all came to enjoy the modern, clean hotels or apartments densely packed into a square mile. These distinct buildings, built by the hundreds between 1935 and 1941 are now known worldwide as Art Deco. The National Register Historic District, as noted in the Miami Design Preservation League's *Art Deco Guide* "is one of the largest" and "one of the youngest" in the United States. Most of these buildings are less than 70 years old.

Their make-up varied from garden style apartments to mini skyscraper hotels, individually each was unique, but collectively they were of a similar scale and complimented their neighbors. Many share details such as cantilever eyebrows, curved façades, wave-inspired wrought iron, colorful terrazzo, and intricate relief work. Every newcomer seemed to demand that their own small studio apartment be complete with a flourish of architecture and style.

After the Second World War, South Beach wasn't "the" place for vacationers any longer. For those with an eye towards the up-to-the-minute discovered newly-built hotels along Collins Avenue to the north. South of Lincoln Road became a last stop for many of those who stayed. Decay set in as the years went by, and the twinkle of the city's eye dimmed as the energy ran out. Historic preservation of the late 1970s led by Barbara Capitman would be a contentious but prevailing issue right up until the 1990s. Proudly, the Miami Beach historic districts have expanded and led to unparalleled economic prosperity. During the 1980s, Cuban Marielitos claimed many apartments for a few hundred bucks a month, sending shockwaves through the social balance. Spanish came to replace Yiddish as the language of the street corner.

Soon, trendsetters and fun-seekers, a cadre of fashion and music industry people, and people with more money than taste, all came to enjoy this sun-splashed resort all to themselves. Lured by Miami Vice and magazine spreads of models posed on Art Deco towers, the neighborhood reawakened and quickly was covered in multitudes of sherbet colored pastels. We only had one high rise then, the South Pointe Tower, and for a short while, South Beach was the paradise of the residents and their friends alone. Gianni Versace would come along in the early 1990s and seemingly give us his nod of approval by purchasing a most magnificent property on Ocean Drive. A flood of tourism, development, and dollars followed the beacon of celebrity and publicity.

During the mid-1990s, the seedy hotels gave up on weekly transients and became boutique properties with white rooms and green apples. The chains disappeared off the front porch furniture. Crack dealing gave way to Dom Perignon. Lincoln Road went from looking like a vacant bowling lane to a café and chain store mall. Its commercialism complete with offices housing entertainment giants such as MTV Latino and Sony Discos. Collins Avenue transformed from a dilapidated residential area to a commanding fashion district. A thriving arts scene emerged, anchored by the Art Center South Florida, The Wolfsonian-FIU, the Bass Museum, the New World Symphony, and the Miami City Ballet. And Ocean Drive was the engine that drove it all. Cafés and nightclubs transformed neglected hotel lobbies into see and be-seen wonder places. Streams of traffic still head there with no apparent destination in mind, and its activity level often stuns even the locals. A palm-lined park to one side with beach goers, rollerbladers, dogs, kites, party tents, sandcastles, and festivals of all kinds. The other side a colorful stretch of umbrellas shading tables with a constant flow of diners and drinkers. There is still nothing as enchanting as watching the moon rise over the palms or seeing humankind's genetic masterpieces strut their stuff. Ocean Drive will always be Miami Beach's street of dreams.

My love of the Beach began in 1991 when I moved into the historic district and helped a preservation-active friend renovate his newly purchased but condemned apartment building. In 1992 he urged me to take a class on tour guiding. I read everything I could find about Miami Beach and soon began touring visitors through the district. I would live there for the next decade and come to know almost every building by name, architect, and date. My friend's political involvement would lead us to debate every new renovation project and we took changes to our built environment personally.

The political and developmental forces have certainly shaped the city in ways our predecessors could not have dreamed. Our audacity to redevelop South Beach with such a magnitude of building scale as no generation before us has done – and none might possibly do again – clearly shows our confidence. Our destination is world renown and longingly sought out by others from every corner of the globe. It is the subject of what appears to be endless reporting and fantastical visions.

The photos of South Beach that Paul has assembled beg us to reflect upon our surroundings as both reality and fantasy. His lens captures the surreal drama of light and shadow, zeroing in on the contrast of building versus sky, or content against a void. Parapets, finials, and façades are all delightful models for the blinding natural sunlight. The photographer is thus given infinite options to create artwork out of architecture, to create concept out of reality. It is what Carl Fisher did about ninety years ago when he built his mansion at Lincoln Road and Collins Avenue. He saw something no one else did, just as Paul has.

Michael Hughes

tour

The pastel colors, the palm trees, the people, the different languages, the hotels, the neon, the architecture, the Latin flavor. . . I love it all!

I always felt that I had left the U.S. when I arrived here – that feeling of exotic atmosphere that one experiences upon leaving their country. But the kick was I didn't need my passport to find this paradise! . . ."Oh beautiful for spacious skies. . ." the best skies are here. . .

The ocean is perhaps what I love most about living here. . .more days than not it's turquoise, my favorite color. Its vastness reminds me of my smallness, and that calms me. The sunsets make splashes of colors that I have never seen with such clarity, and our moon over the water is more beautiful than anywhere I've ever been.

What privilege to be a resident in a place where people the world over want to vacation!

Iris Chase

"Cloudy Ocean Drive"

"Carlysle"

"Essex House"

"Balcony"

"Netherland"

"Post Office"

"Victor Silhouette"

"Palm Star"

classic

I've been living here now for nine years, in total bliss! The beauty of the light really appeals to me. As a painter, this is the perfect setting for my creativity.

The light makes me feel like I'm sitting in the lap of Heaven! Beautiful. . .and the ocean, serene and mystifying, as blue as the sky.

The people, multicultural, warm, and friendly, welcoming you unconditionally into their town.

And this book allows everyone to experience, through its unique photographs the magic of this place.

Thanks Paul, for creating this opportunity for us to celebrate and express our feelings about South Beach.

Helene Weiss

"Delano"

"Ritz"

"Shelborne"

"Loews"

"St. Moritz"

"Albion"

new

South Beach inspires! Living in the conservative environment of my hometown was somewhat limiting. At times it seemed like a slow, spiritual death. However, the energy of South Beach made me come alive!

Freedom through expression can be empowering. This town allows you to be yourself, to make the most of who you are, giving you the ability to realize your potential!

It's full of individuals who encompass these qualities and intoxicating creative energy! It is wonderful to be part of a place that has this kind of effect on people.

Stephen Anderson

"Skew"

"Cubist II"

"Royal Plaza"

"1017 Close-up"

"1017"

"Reach"

lincoln

I stood on the 1000 block of Lincoln Road in 1993 and wondered if anyone would ever even walk by the new business I was about to open. On that pedestrian street, who would understand, want, and be able to buy good design? I had a dream and I only wanted to live it in South Beach.

As I see it, we have it all on South Beach. You can tune into whatever level you choose – be it nightlife, beach, the arts, or business. And the best part is you can jump from one activity to the other nearly any day of the week! Not surprisingly, many New Yorkers are flocking here at every chance they have, and if we can attract such a discriminating crowd, it is very telling of how far we've come.

Dreams do come true and a few years ago I was even able to move here, where I found my sense of community, socially and professionally. No more suburbs for me! I may not have been born in Miami Beach, but this is my home in every sense of the word for me.

Daniel Bowman

"Movies"

"Metal Fins"

"Fissure"

"Balls"

"Diamonds"

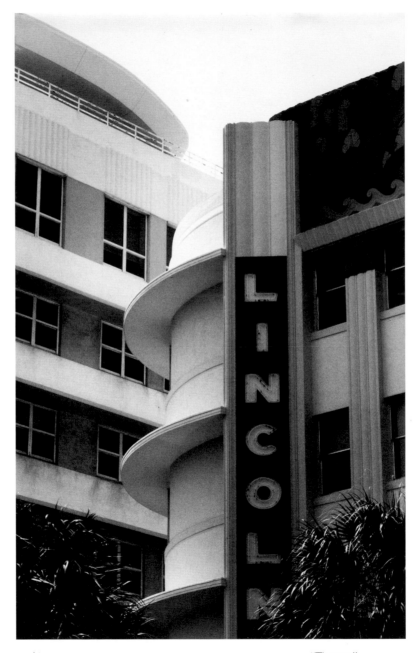

"Theater"

lush

Found the land so lush and porous
and the dreams were living for us
found the stars so bright and many
and the hopes shined bright off any

Mauricio Barrera

"Lush"

"Sundrenched"

"Urban Planter"

"Delano Pool"

wave

Most cities erect monuments to great heroes,

and build skyscrapers

that represent worldly accomplishments.

We emigrate from cities and towns

that urge us to labor and achieve.

With the first glance of vast blue sky

and inviting ocean waters, however,

one releases the past and begins anew.

Our architecture mirrors sunrises,

ocean tides, and sweeping sands.

We live here in the playful reminder

not to take ourselves too seriously.

Here, we learn not to just strive,

but to simply be.

Asandra

"Sinuous Rooftop"

"Sweeping Canopy"

"Wavy Wall"

"Shady Composition"

sculptural

one line and shadow
grabs the moment to stop me
as pink sun hangs the moon

Cora Bettcher

"Palette Vertical"

"Palette"

"Wave"

"Plaid"

"Take-off"

"Fancy"

abstract

here at the edge of a continent. . .
past dreams propel future realities
present cultures and ideas collide
under an expansive sky
sparking dreams and desires to build
like billowing cumulus
into thunderheads
breaking open –
heavy with possibility
to wash the streets
and drench the steamy nights
with an energy alive
and an infinite opportunity
to create –
anything
everything
here at the edge. . .

Julie Davidow

"Metal Steps"

"Below Polygon"

"Facing Polygon"

"Dialogue"

"Tic-Tac-Toe"

"Pollock Window"

detail

The winter of 1992 was bitterly cold. I had closed my Soho gallery and moved to my house in Southampton to figure out the next phase of my life. I remember short, dark, windy, icy days when I would spend hours at a time under the electric blanket fantasizing about living in the tropics. One day my New York Magazine arrived with a cover story on South Beach, calling it something like the "Prozac of Cities." I put the house up for sale and by August found myself living the dream.

My earliest memories of South Beach entail floating in the hot, turquoise sea at sunset, watching the Deco buildings on Ocean Drive gradually light up as the sky darkened, and thinking I was finally in paradise. Weeks later came Hurricane Andrew, and in the years following, some personal hurricanes of my own. But every time I travel, I find myself looking forward to returning to the now-familiar and comforting, warm blanket of humidity that pervades the atmosphere of South Beach.

Bianca Lanza

"Sun"

"Light Carving"

"Floral Concrete"

"Shield"

"Frieze"

"Stepped Relief"

home

The way the branches of these overpowering trees cover me out here, the way the humid air embraces me so fully and my nostrils drink the night dew of calm and warmth of life, and the way I recall the days and the nights out here, resemble in my heart happiness. It is out here that I have felt, and it is under these vaults of green, at times heavy with warm rain as droplets fall from leaf to limb to leaf to ground, the pieces of my life come together to one, whole, grounded me.

Storms have shaken me and I have ridden them, helped by those green beings protecting me with their steadfastly shivering leaves suspended in nightly air – wet and warm all around me – I look up into the deep and hear the thousands of speaking birds, the only sound to be heard out here on this island just before dawn, in that softest hour of all hours – all except you – quiet and peaceful, you tree full of life and love and lingering light of days that ended in darkness as dark as this day is light down here, out here far from home, yet with all you gave me, home – now.

Johan Blom

"Going Up"

"West Side Story"

"Marina"

"Side"

"White Balconies"

"One Hundred"

night

There's a nightclub in South Beach to suit every kind of taste! The clubs here offer the opportunity to experience the most diverse music, especially with a Latin flavor. Even if one is not familiar with the Latin rhythms, South Beach is very laid back and you can find yourself learning to dance salsa or merengue. It doesn't matter if you go clubbing Monday, Tuesday, or any other night of the week – you are sure to have a night to remember! Unforgettable clubs, unforgettable people! And after indulging in dancing the night away, you can always finish off with a great slice of pizza on Washington Avenue.

James Mckenzie

"Neon Ocean Drive"

"Neon Canopies"

"Contour"

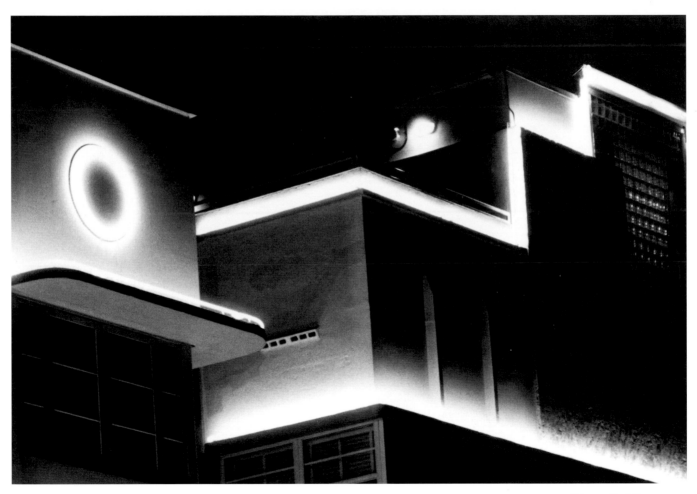

"Neon Circle"

"Cameo"

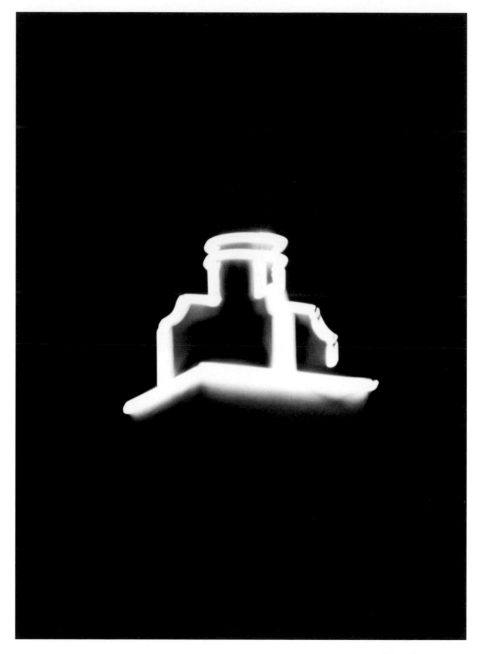

"Neon"

photo locations

"Tides Side"
Ocean Drive and 12th Street

"Essex House"
Collins Avenue
and 10th Street

"Cloudy Ocean Drive"
Ocean Drive from the
beach at 12th Street

"Balcony"
Ocean Drive and 13th Street

"Carlysle"
Ocean Drive and 13th Street

"Netherland"
Ocean Drive and 13th Street

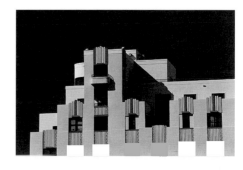

"Post Office"
Washington Avenue
and 13th Street

"Delano"
Collins Avenue and 17th Street

"Victor Silhouette"
Ocean Drive and 12th Street

"Ritz"
Collins Avenue and 17th Street

"Palm Star"
Ocean Drive and 12th Street

"Shelborne"
Collins Avenue
and 18th Street

"Loews"
Collins Avenue and 16th Street

"Skew"
Washington
Avenue and 3rd Street

"St Moritz"
Collins Avenue
and 16th Street

"Cubist II"
Washington
Avenue and 2nd Street

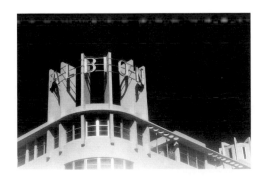

"Albion"
Lincoln Road and
James Avenue

"Royal Plaza"
Collins Avenue and 16th Street

"1017 Close-up"
1017 Meridian Avenue

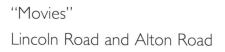

"Movies"
Lincoln Road and Alton Road

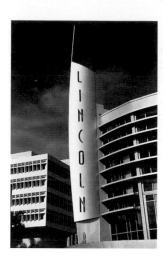

"1017"
1017 Meridian Avenue

"Metal Fins"
Lincoln Road
and Meridian Avenue

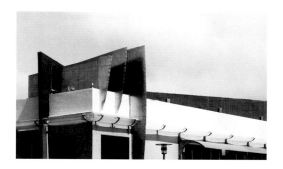

"Reach"
Ocean Drive and 15th Street

"Fissure"
Lincoln Road and Meridian Avenue

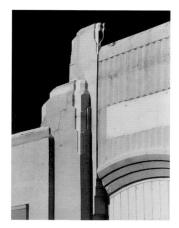

"Balls"
Lincoln Road and
Pennsylvania Avenue

"Lush"
Michigan Avenue
and 4th Street

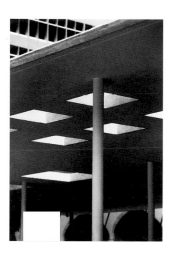

"Diamonds"
Lincoln Road and Lenox Avenue

"Sundrenched"
Meridian Avenue and 10th Street

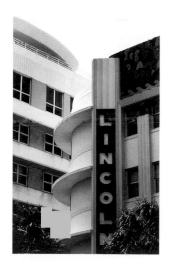

"Theater"
Lincoln Road and Pennsylvania Avenue

"Urban Planter"
Lincoln Road, seen from above

"Delano Pool"
Beach and 17th
Street, Delano Hotel

"Wavy Wall"
Washington
Avenue and 11th Street

"Sinuous Rooftop"
Michigan Avenue
and 5th Street

"Shady Composition"
Washington Avenue and 11th Street

"Sweeping Canopy"
Lincoln Road
and Lenox Avenue

"Palette Vertical"
Beach at 15th Street

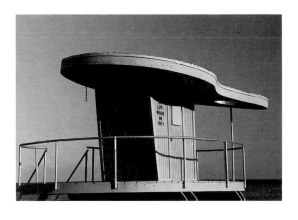

"Palette"
Beach at 15th Street

"Take-off"
Beach at 12th Street

"Wave"
Beach at 8th Street

"Fancy"
Beach at 3rd Street

"Plaid"
Beach at 12th Street

"Metal Steps"
Lincoln Road
and Meridian Avenue

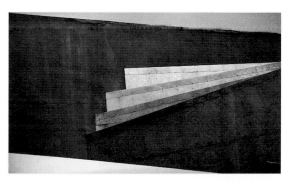

"Below Polygon"
Meridian Court and 9th Street

"Tic-Tac-Toe"
Ocean Drive and 12th Street

"Facing Polygon"
Meridian Court and 9th Street

"Pollock Window"
Michigan Avenue
and 9th Street

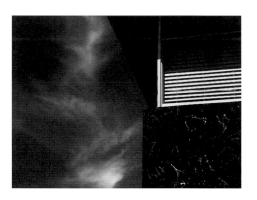

"Dialogue"
Meridian Court
and 9th Street

"Sun"
Jefferson Avenue
and 9th Street

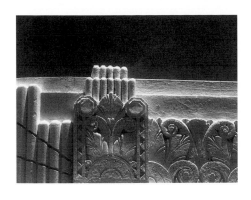

"Light Carving"
Washington
Avenue and 6th Street

"Frieze"
Washington
Avenue and 10th Street

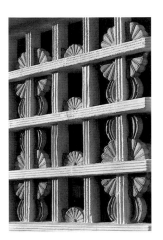

"Floral Concrete"
Ocean Drive and 15th Street

"Stepped Relief"
Washington Avenue and 4th Street

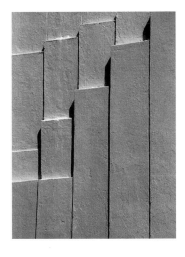

"Shield"
Washington Avenue and 10th Street

"Going Up"
South of 5th Street, seen
from Government Cut

"West Side Story"
West Avenue,
seen from Biscayne Bay

"White Balconies"
Lincoln Road
and Collins Avenue

"Marina"
Alton Road, South
of 5th Street, seen
from Government Cut

"One Hundred"
Lincoln Road and Collins Avenue

"Side"
100 Lincoln Road

"Neon Ocean Drive"
Ocean Drive and 14th Street

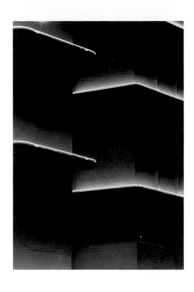

"Neon Canopies"
Ocean Drive and 14th Street

"Cameo"
Washington Avenue
and Espanola Way

"Neon Circle"
Ocean Drive and 14th Street

"Contour"
Washington Avenue and 15th Street

"Neon"
Collins Avenue and 14th Street

contributors

Foreword — Michael Hughes is a New England native and has lived in Miami since 1987. He began as a volunteer guide for the Miami Design Preservation League in 1992 and was named tour guide of the year in 1996 and 2000. In 1997 he joined the Wolfsonian-Florida International University as visitor services manager. In 2000, he began studying for a degree in history at FIU, focusing on South Florida.

Tour — Iris Chase is a jewelry designer and a resident artist.

Classic — Helene Weiss is an artist, an accomplished painter originally from New York City.

New — Stephen Anderson has found total freedom in South Beach.

Lincoln — Daniel Bowman is one of South Beach's pioneer retailers, responsible for making it such a sophisticated and trendy shopping destination.

Lush — Mauricio Barrera is a supporter, enthusiast, and active participant in the visual arts.

Wave — Asandra is a fine artist and metaphysician. Her art has been greatly influenced by the brilliance and humor of the Southern Florida landscape.

Sculptural — Cora Bettcher has operated contemporary fine art galleries in Miami and South Beach since 1995. She blissfully resides in Miami Beach, and is currently single.

Abstract — Julie Davidow/artist/Miami native/South Beach resident since 1985.

Detail — Bianca Lanza is an art dealer and museum store consultant. She is originally from New York.

Home — Johan Blom is a psychology professional who enjoys writing in his free time.

Night — James Mckenzie was born in Virginia, grew up in Colombia, and now enjoys the nightlife in South Beach.